Reading Is the Key !!

EXPLORING THE
DEPTHS OF THE OCEAN

by Todd Kortemeier

12 STORY LIBRARY

www.12StoryLibrary.com

Copyright © 2017 by Peterson Publishing Company, North Mankato, MN 56003. All rights reserved. No part of this book may be reproduced or utilized in any form or by any means without written permission from the publisher.

12-Story Library is an imprint of Peterson Publishing Company and Press Room Editions.

Produced for 12-Story Library by Red Line Editorial

Photographs ©: Dudarev Mikhail/Shutterstock Images, cover, 1; Ray Grinaway/Thinkstock, 4; Tero Hakala/Shutterstock Images, 6; Arsgera/Shutterstock Images, 7, 29; Art Howard/NOAA Ocean Exploration and Research, 8; NOAA Office of Ocean Exploration, 9; VanderWolf Images/Shutterstock Images, 10; Scott Roth/Invision/AP Images, 11; Tane Casserley/NOAA/MONITOR NMS, 12; Julian Kutzim/Picture-Alliance/DPA/AP Images, 13; Ethan Daniels/Shutterstock Images, 14; NOAA Ship David Starr Jordan Collection; Commander John Herring, NOAA Corps, 15; NOAA Okeanos Explorer Program, 16; f11photo/Shutterstock Images, 17, 28; Robert Schwemmer/CINMS/NOAA, 18; David Burdick/NOAA, 19; NSF/NOAA, 20; Haris Vythoulkas/Shutterstock Images, 22; NASA, 23; Alex Mit/Shutterstock Images, 24; NOAA NESDIS Environmental Visualization Laboratory, 25; Jacques Rougerie/SeaOrbiter/Rex Features/AP Images, 27

Library of Congress Cataloging-in-Publication Data
Cataloging-in-publication information is on file with the Library of Congress.
978-1-63235-377-1 (hardcover)
978-1-63235-394-8 (paperback)
978-1-62143-518-1 (hosted ebook)

Printed in the United States of America
Mankato, MN
May, 2016

Access free, up-to-date content on this topic plus a full digital version of this book. Scan the QR code on page 31 or use your school's login at 12StoryLibrary.com.

Table of Contents

The Ocean Is the Last Frontier 4

The Ocean Is Full of Extremes 6

Research Ships Are Floating Laboratories 8

Submersibles Go Deeper Than Ever 10

Divers Can Explore Shallow Depths 12

Observation Systems Monitor the Oceans 14

Strange Creatures Live in the Deep Ocean 16

Shipwrecks Litter the Deep 18

Underwater Volcanoes Change Earth's Surface 20

Underwater Cities, the Past and Our Future 22

Ocean Currents Are a Possible Energy Source 24

The SeaOrbiter Is an Oceangoing Spaceship 26

Fact Sheet 28

Glossary 30

For More Information 31

Index 32

About the Author 32

1

The Ocean Is the Last Frontier

For thousands of years, people have sailed Earth's oceans. But what lies below the surface has long remained a mystery. Ancient Viking sailors took the first steps to finding out in the 700s. They dropped weights off a long line of ships into the ocean. Then they pulled them back up and used the arm span of a sailor to see how deep it was. This distance was about six feet (1.8 m), and is still used today. It is called a fathom.

The weights also brought up samples of the soft dirt from the ocean bottom. The Viking sailors had no way to analyze these samples.

The Vikings were the first known people to explore below the ocean's surface.

4

MAPPING THE OCEAN FLOOR

Earth's oceans are wide, deep, and hard to map. There are maps of the ocean floor, but not in great detail. Only objects in the ocean larger than 3.1 miles (5 km) are completely mapped. There are planets that have more detailed maps. Mars has been mapped to within 328 feet (100 m).

But it was an early clue into what is beneath the waves. Those depths remained a mystery for many years. In the 1870s, a ship called the HMS *Challenger* made the first significant exploration of the seafloor. The ship traveled nearly 70,000 miles (113,000 km) around the world. Its crew mapped underwater features using a similar method to the Vikings. They also discovered new species of life that they brought on board.

It was not until the 1930s that humans got to actually see the ocean floor. New submarines were able to dive thousands of feet. In 1960, humans visited the very bottom of the ocean. The *Trieste* took two people to Challenger Deep in the Mariana Trench, 35,810 feet (10,915 m) below the surface of the Pacific Ocean.

The ocean covers most of Earth. But there is still a lot we do not know about it. As technology advances, scientists are finding out more about oceans every day.

5
Thickness, in inches (13 cm), of the metal walls of the *Trieste* needed to withstand the pressure of the Challenger Deep.

- The Vikings were the first to try to measure the ocean depth.
- They brought up samples of soft dirt from the ocean floor.
- The HMS *Challenger* made an important ocean exploration voyage in the 1870s.
- In 1960, humans visited Challenger Deep, the deepest point on Earth.

5

The Ocean Is Full of Extremes

The ocean takes up a large portion of Earth's surface. Yet it has barely been explored. One reason for this is simply its size. Ocean water covers more than 129 million square miles (334 million sq. km) of Earth. The ocean is an extreme environment. It is a tough place to explore.

At 650 feet (200 m) below the water's surface, it gets very dark. At 13,000 feet (3,960 m) deep, the water temperature is freezing. There is no sunlight at this depth. But the ocean goes way deeper than that. The deepest parts of the ocean are in the Mariana Trench in the Pacific Ocean. Its deepest point, Challenger Deep, is lower than Mount Everest is tall.

At this depth, there is intense pressure. Without special equipment, humans are not able to dive deeper than 165 feet (50 m). Only three people have ever been to Challenger Deep.

> It is difficult for scientists to explore the oceans because they are so vast.

A NATIONAL MONUMENT

The Mariana Trench is near the island of Guam in the Pacific Ocean. Because Guam is a territory of the United States, the United States oversees the Mariana Trench. The Mariana Trench Marine National Monument was established in 2009. This allows the National Wildlife Refuge System to help protect this unique part of Earth.

For these reasons, it may not be a surprise that explorers have seen only five percent of the ocean.

71
Percent of Earth covered by ocean, making up 97 percent of all water on the planet.

- Earth's surface is mostly covered by ocean.
- The ocean is very hard to explore for several reasons.
- Ocean water becomes too dark to see as you get deeper.
- High pressures mean only special equipment can survive certain depths.

Earth's highest mountain, Mount Everest, is more than 29,000 feet (8,800 m) above sea level.

3

Research Ships Are Floating Laboratories

Because of the size of the oceans, exploring them means going a long distance. Scientists work thousands of miles offshore. But they still need all their equipment. The ships they use have to be many things at once. They provide a home for the crew. They carry all the food and water everyone needs. And they must have the lab space to work on the go.

The National Oceanic and Atmospheric Administration (NOAA) operates the *Okeanos Explorer*. It is 224 feet (68 m) long, and first belonged to the US Navy. The *Okeanos Explorer*'s mission is to discover as much about the ocean as possible.

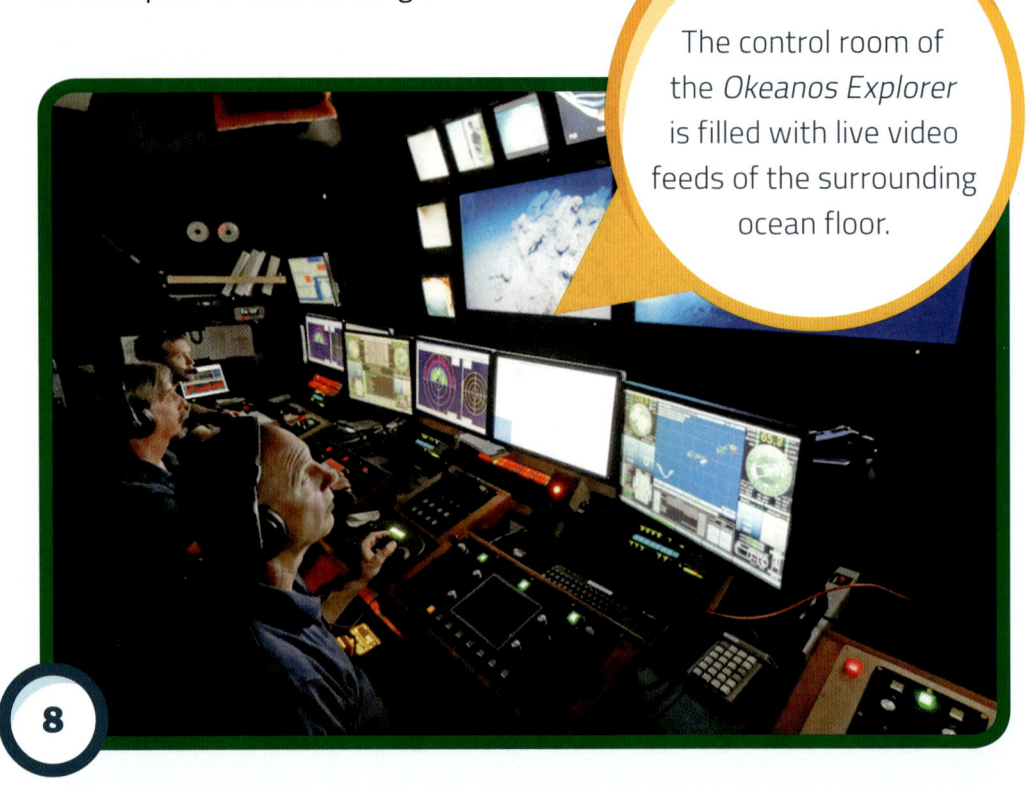

The control room of the *Okeanos Explorer* is filled with live video feeds of the surrounding ocean floor.

Two NOAA scientists recover *Alvin* after a mission before bringing it back to *Atlantis*.

This ship has one big advantage. Not all the scientists on the study need to be on board during a voyage. The ship has state-of-the-art technology to transmit data back to shore. It also can stream images over the Internet. The ship carries robots that dive thousands of feet below the water's surface. These robots have powerful lights, cameras, and sensors to collect data.

The research ship *Atlantis* belongs to the US Navy. The Woods Hole Oceanographic Institute uses it for research. *Atlantis* has more than 3,500 square feet (325 sq. m) of lab space. It can host a crew of 24 scientists for up to 60 days at sea. *Atlantis* is also capable of launching its own submersible, *Alvin*. A submersible is a special kind of submarine. It is smaller and relies on another ship to launch it. *Alvin* can take a small crew to some of the deepest parts of the ocean.

274

Length, in feet (84 m), of the *Ronald H. Brown*, the largest ship in the NOAA fleet.

- Research ships carry all the equipment for scientists working out in the ocean.
- The *Okeanos Explorer* can send data back to shore for scientists working there.
- It can also stream images over the Internet.
- The *Atlantis* can launch a submersible from its deck.

4

Submersibles Go Deeper Than Ever

Without special equipment, humans can dive only 165 feet (50m) underwater. To go deeper, humans sometimes use submersibles that carry only a few people. These vessels are specially designed to hold up under the pressure of deep water.

Submarines are an old idea. Dutch inventor Cornelius Drebbel created the first one. He demonstrated it for the King of England in the 1600s. Drebbel's submarine could only dive approximately 15 feet (4.6 m). Current submersibles that can hit depths of more than 30,000 feet (9,100 m) have been around since the 1960s.

Alvin has been exploring the sea since 1964. It can dive nearly 15,000 feet (4,570 m) deep. It can carry three people. *Alvin* has made more than 4,500 dives carrying 13,000 people since it was built. The little sub has seen some amazing sights. In 1966, it located a lost bomb from World War II (1939–1945). In 1986, it visited the wreck of the RMS *Titanic*, which sank in 1912.

The *Deepsea Challenger* is the latest and greatest in sub technology.

> The military has used submarines for years.

10

In 2012, it carried a person to Challenger Deep for the first time since the *Trieste* did in 1960. It took more than two and a half hours to reach the bottom. Unlike *Trieste*, *Deepsea Challenger* was able to take many pictures. It has eight high-definition cameras.

There are also unmanned subs that operate remotely. These have the same diving capabilities as manned ones. The deep ocean can be a dangerous place. Unmanned subs put no human lives at risk.

$30,000
Cost per day to operate *Alvin*.

- The first submarine was invented in the 1600s.
- *Alvin* has made many important discoveries since launching in 1964.
- *Deepsea Challenger* can dive deeper than any other sub.
- Scientists operate unmanned subs remotely.

The *Deepsea Challenger* has arms that can take samples from the seafloor for analysis.

5

Divers Can Explore Shallow Depths

Human divers are great at exploring things underwater. They can swim into small areas. They also can use their hands to pick up objects or hold tools. In shallower waters, divers are better explorers than robots. Basic diving equipment includes an air tank. How long a diver can spend underwater varies. It depends on how deep the dive is and how fast the diver breathes.

Divers are not advised to go any deeper than 130 feet (40 m). Going deeper can be dangerous. Any equipment failure leaves you with little time to get help. And people can get sick if they swim to the water's surface too quickly.

But knowing these risks has not stopped people from trying to dive deep. Divers with no special equipment have gone more than 1,000 feet (305 m) deep. They have to train for decades to be able to attempt such a deep dive. In 2014, Ahmed Gabr broke a world record by diving 1,090 feet (332 m). But he did it with many air tanks and help from other divers.

Divers need special equipment to dive much deeper than normal. Pressure suits can protect a person

Scuba divers must go through training to learn how to properly dive.

12

14
Number of hours it took Ahmed Gabr to safely return to the surface after his record dive.

- Diving is a great way to explore things up close.
- Divers cannot safely go more than 130 feet (40 m) down.
- Special suits made to withstand pressure and provide breathable air can greatly increase a diver's time and depth in the water.
- The Exosuit allows a diver to go down 1,000 feet (300 m) for 50 hours.

from the pressure of the deep ocean. The Exosuit costs $600,000 and can take a person 1,000 feet (300 m) underwater. The pressure feels normal for the diver inside.

The Exosuit weighs 530 pounds (240 kg). Though the suit is big, divers can still easily pick up objects. One use scientists have planned for the suit is studying certain fish up close. Fish that glow underwater are called bioluminescent. These fish are hard to bring up to the surface. If they survive, they do not always glow. Finding out what makes them glow could be useful in medical research for humans.

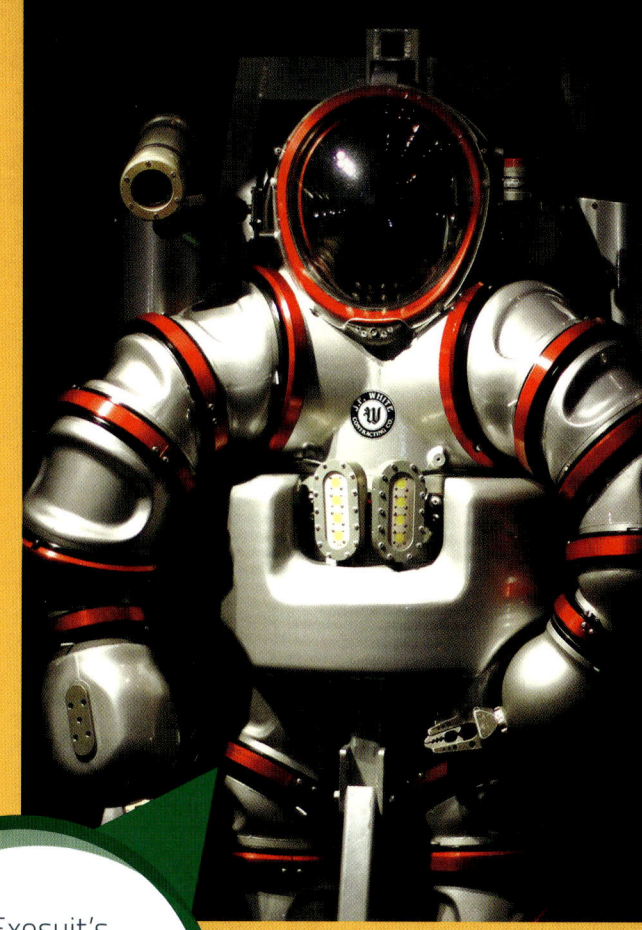

The Exosuit's life support system gives a diver 50 hours of breathable air in the water.

13

6 Observation Systems Monitor the Oceans

Science has developed a lot in the last 50 years. Technology now exists to monitor the world's oceans from anywhere. Data about the oceans can be used to predict weather around Earth.

The way oceans flow is called the current. Ocean currents can influence weather patterns anywhere on Earth. Scientists place devices called drifters around the globe to monitor currents. They work simply. They have four pieces of fabric that catch moving water. This turns a tube and relays the water speed. Drifters can detect which way a weather system might be moving.

But observation systems do not need to be in the water. They do not even need to be on this planet. Satellites can observe oceans from space. They can zoom in on a few miles of ocean, or see up to 1,500 miles (2,414 km). These

Ocean currents tend to leave patterns on the seafloor.

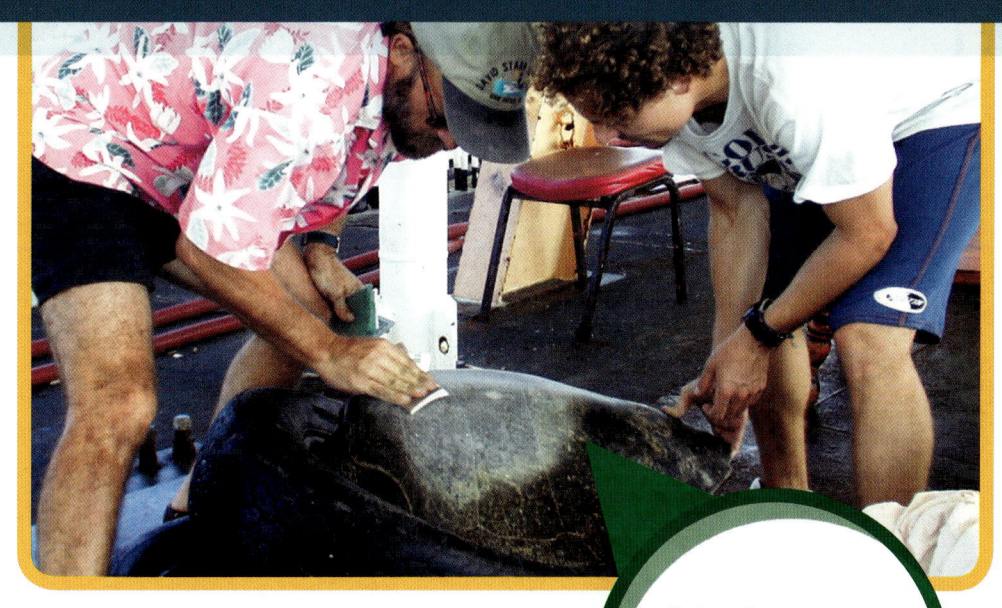

Scientists prep a sea turtle to have a satellite tracking device attached.

satellites also monitor ocean temperature. The ocean temperature can affect the formation of weather and the behavior of sea life.

Satellites are also used for mapping. They are able to detect shallow objects such as coral reefs. The satellites take pictures of the same area regularly. This helps scientists detect any changes in the reefs.

Even animals can help study the ocean. Scientists from NOAA place sensors on the shells of sea turtles. These sensors relay ocean temperature, depth, and the location of the turtle. This data can then be combined with what satellites observe. This data together helps give an overall picture of ocean conditions.

500
Distance, in miles (800 km), above Earth that satellites fly in orbit.

- Scientists today can observe the ocean remotely.
- Drifters measure currents, which can help predict the weather.
- Satellites observe oceans from space.
- Sensors placed on sea life work together with satellite data.

7

Strange Creatures Live in the Deep Ocean

It takes a special kind of creature to survive and thrive in the deep ocean. The darkness, the freezing cold water, and the pressure make it a tough place to live. Very little of the ocean floor has been explored. It is hard to say how many never-before-seen species are down there.

At seven miles (11 km) below the surface, it might seem like nothing could live in the Mariana Trench. But scientists have found quite the opposite. Sending a crew down is very difficult. Instead, scientists send down packages of instruments and cameras that they operate remotely. However, the pressure at that depth is so strong that sometimes the packages are crushed.

With these instruments, scientists can observe the deepest-dwelling fish ever seen. These fish do not look much like other fish. They have nearly clear skin and a body like an eel. They are a new species of snailfish. Scientists have found other new species, too, including some tiny shrimplike creatures.

Some deep-sea fish, such as tonguefish, are flat so they can easily grab food from the seafloor.

THINK ABOUT IT

Animals that live in the deep ocean need special adaptations to live there. What other animals are adapted to their environment? Are there similar features in humans?

98
Percent of the ocean's species that live on or close to the seafloor.

- Creatures must be highly adapted to surviving in the deep ocean.
- Scientists have discovered many species that live in the very deepest part of the ocean.
- Fish at that depth contain a chemical that lets them survive the high pressure.
- The ocean is so big that many species have not been discovered yet.

The fish contain a chemical in their bodies that help them live at these depths. It keeps their bodies flexible so they can withstand the crushing pressure. The fish cannot survive being brought to the water's surface.

There are other creatures that live in somewhat shallower water. The giant spider crab lives at approximately 1,000 feet (300 m). There is also the frilled shark. It is called a living fossil because its relatives lived during the dinosaur era. The frilled shark lives at up to 5,000 feet (1,524 m) deep.

The giant spider crab looks similar to a regular crab but can be 12 feet (3.7 m) wide.

Shipwrecks Litter the Deep

Since the invention of the ship, there have been shipwrecks. Man has been sailing Earth's oceans for thousands of years. Ships sometimes run into things. Or they sink during storms or wars. However it happens, shipwrecks litter the bottom of the ocean.

Shipwrecks have a lot of historical value. By exploring them, we can learn what life was like at the time the ship sank. Some shipwrecks are found by accident. Fishermen may get their nets caught in one. But sometimes explorers set out looking for a particular wreck. This search can take years. Even if people know where a ship went down, the water could be very deep. Or the ship could have drifted miles underwater.

The RMS *Titanic* was a famous ship that sank in 1912. People knew where it sank in the north Atlantic Ocean. But it took more than 70 years to find. The ship was in very deep water, approximately 2.5 miles (4 km) down. Scientists used sonar to find it. Sonar uses sound to find underwater objects. The wreck was discovered in 1985. The next year, people laid eyes on *Titanic* for the first time since 1912

There are millions of shipwrecks on the seafloor for divers and scientists to explore.

through the windows of the *Alvin* submersible.

In 2015, the wreck of the Spanish sailing ship *San Jose* was discovered off the coast of Colombia. It sank during a sea battle in 1708. This ship was built in 1696, making it more than 300 years old. The *San Jose* still contained billions of dollars worth of gold and silver.

Divers sometimes explore wrecks in shallower water. Some of these wrecks are protected because they are important evidence from history. Sometimes, very old wrecks are home to living coral. These are called artificial coral reefs.

Divers must take care not to disturb the coral growing on shipwrecks.

THE FILMMAKER AND EXPLORER

James Cameron is a movie director. He directed a movie about the *Titanic* in 1997. He also is an underwater explorer. He piloted *Deepsea Challenger* to the deepest point in the ocean in 2012. He was the third person to make it to the bottom of the Mariana Trench.

3 million
Estimated number of shipwrecks on the ocean floor.

- Some shipwrecks are thousands of years old.
- Some shipwrecks are discovered accidentally, but others are searched for.
- It took more than 70 years to find the wreck of the *Titanic* in very deep water.
- Divers can explore wrecks but must not do damage.

9

Underwater Volcanoes Change Earth's Surface

Earth's surface may look fairly stable. But far beneath our feet, it is always changing. Volcanoes are signs of these changes. Underwater volcanoes change the look of the seafloor when they erupt. These volcanoes are much more active than those on land. The most active ones are an average of 8,500 feet (2,600 m) below the surface.

THE THREAT OF ERUPTIONS

Though occurring deep underwater, eruptions can still do damage. A volcano shoots out very hot rocks. These rocks can go miles through the water. They can hit ships and sink them. The waves an eruption makes could also cause a tsunami. This is a huge wave that does damage when it hits land.

Underwater volcanic eruptions are much harder to monitor than those above ground.

There are approximately one million volcanoes underwater. Though they can be huge in size, some are still being discovered. In 2015, scientists accidentally discovered four volcanoes off the coast of Australia while studying lobsters in the area. The largest was nearly one mile (1.6 km) wide and more than 2,290 feet (700 m) high.

Even with so many volcanoes, underwater eruptions are hard to spot. There have been nearly 8,000 eruptions observed on Earth in the last 10,000 years. Only around 300 are known to be underwater. There must be a lot of eruptions that scientists cannot see. Either the volcanoes are too deep, or the ocean is too big.

Scientists look for evidence of eruptions. When volcanoes spew lava, the surrounding water cools it immediately. This makes new land formations in the water. The water surrounding the lava is much warmer than normal right after an eruption.

Sometimes sea life moves into these new spaces. Some species thrive in the warm waters. Eruptions give off minerals that some sea life need to survive.

75,000
Number of known underwater volcanoes that stand at least 0.5 miles (0.8 km) off the seafloor.

- Volcanoes are more active underwater than on land.
- There are approximately one million underwater volcanoes, some of which are very large.
- Eruptions are hard to detect in progress.
- Lava flows harden and change the look of the seafloor after an eruption.

THINK ABOUT IT
A lot of volcanoes are located where earthquakes are more likely. Why do you think this is? How might the two be related?

10 Underwater Cities, the Past and Our Future

A shipwreck can have great historical value. It shows what life was like at the time that ship sank. But nothing captures that better than an entire sunken city. As the geography of Earth changes, locations sometimes sink underwater. The sunken cities discovered now were last above water thousands of years ago.

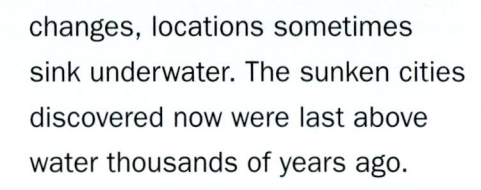

The Greek philosopher Plato wrote about an island city called Atlantis. He said it sank into the ocean more than 10,000 years before our time. Scientists have long searched for what might have been Atlantis. Every sunken city discovered could have been the famous lost city.

> Plato is one of the most widely read philosophers.

THE UNDERWATER LAB

The National Aeronautics and Space Administration (NASA) operates an underwater training base in Florida. The station is located 3.5 miles (5.6 km) off the coast and 62 feet (19 m) below the surface. The base simulates what it is like to be isolated in space. Astronauts and other researchers stay there for up to three weeks.

The underwater NASA team works on space drills on the seafloor.

In 2015, archaeologists found an underwater city off the coast of Greece. Divers found a few pieces of broken pottery. It was the first clue as to what lay beneath. They soon found the ruins of buildings. There were paved streets. More pottery and evidence of tools lay all over. But it is not likely to be Atlantis. It is only approximately 4,500 years old.

In the future, some people may live in cities actually built underwater. Japanese architects have designed a city that would float below the surface. Most of its interior space would be contained inside a big glass bubble. The giant globe would have businesses and homes for 5,000 people. The technology to build this place does not exist yet. But the firm believes it could be constructed as soon as 2035.

1,640
Diameter, in feet (500 m), of Japan's proposed underwater city.

- Some ancient cities have been covered in water over time.
- These cities are well-preserved examples of what life was like back then.
- These cities are thousands of years old.
- In the future, modern cities may be constructed underwater.

11

Ocean Currents Are a Possible Energy Source

The ocean is always moving. Similar to the wind, if the ocean's movement could be captured, it would make a good source of energy. Water carries much more energy than air. Water moving 12 miles per hour (19 km/h) has the same force as a 110-mile-per-hour (177-km/h) wind. Ocean turbine technology is still in the early stages. But it has a lot of potential. Capturing even a small portion of the ocean's potential would make a lot of energy. Such a system would work similar to the way a wind turbine does. Moving water would turn a set of blades. That turning motion would generate electricity. Researchers must first find the best place to put these machines. Then they have to figure out how to get the electricity to homes and businesses on land.

So far, only a few tests have been carried out. But the technology is promising. A single turbine 100 feet (30 m) across could power 13,500 homes. Wind turbines that are bigger than that power only about 240 homes. Only small real-world examples of a water turbine exist. A single turbine near Scotland produced power for 500 homes in 2012. Other tests are ongoing near Florida.

Ocean turbines are just starting to be tested.

Ocean wind has the potential to be used as an alternative energy source.

Scientists must take care not to disrupt the ocean environment. There is sea life that could be affected by large machines. If currents are interrupted, it could have an effect on weather patterns. More research is needed. But the ocean could be a reliable source of energy in the future.

3.8 million
Number of homes that could be powered by the currents surrounding the state of Florida.

- Ocean currents are always moving.
- That movement could be captured as energy just like the wind.
- Ocean currents are much more powerful than the wind.
- Harvesting current energy could have negative impacts on the environment.

12

The SeaOrbiter Is an Oceangoing Spaceship

If it were not floating in the water, you could mistake the SeaOrbiter for a spaceship. And in some ways, it has a lot in common with the International Space Station. Both help scientists explore new and strange environments. Under construction since 2014, the SeaOrbiter will one day let scientists see the ocean as never before. A nonstop study of the ocean has never been done.

Most of the SeaOrbiter will be underwater. This will allow divers to go deeper more easily. For deeper dives, it also will have robots and submersibles it can launch. Some of these will go nearly 20,000 feet (6,100 m) deep. It also will have plenty of space for lab experiments.

The ship will not do any damage to the environment, either. It will operate on solar and wind energy. Electric engines will power it. That means SeaOrbiter will never run out of fuel. Scientists will be able to live on board. Research will never end. A crew of up to 22 people can live on it.

The SeaOrbiter will help bring the ocean to others. It will be equipped

101.7

Length, in feet (31 m), of the SeaOrbiter below the surface. It will be 88.6 feet (27 m) above it.

- The SeaOrbiter is a ship designed to explore the ocean.
- People will live on board and study the sea long-term.
- It will have submersibles on board that can dive almost 20,000 feet (6,100 m).
- It can broadcast information about the ocean around the world.

with a broadcast studio. The ship and its crew will be able to communicate with people all over the world.

The SeaOrbiter is estimated to cost $43 million to build.

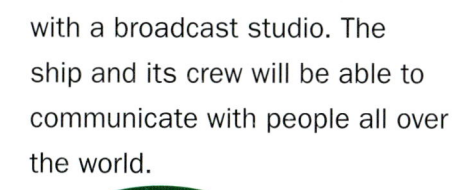

THINK ABOUT IT

Would you want to live at sea? What do you think would be the hardest part? What would you take with you on your voyage?

Fact Sheet

- The Pacific Ocean is the biggest ocean. It takes up 30 percent of Earth's surface. It also has the most islands: 25,000. The Atlantic Ocean is the second largest. It takes up 21 percent of Earth's surface. Third is the Indian Ocean, at 14 percent. If all the water in the oceans were put into a cube, it would need to have sides 600 miles (1,000 km) long.

- Most countries now recognize the Southern Ocean as the Earth's fifth ocean. It used to be considered part of the Arctic Ocean, the smallest ocean. However the boundaries of the Southern Ocean are not agreed upon.

- The average depth of the ocean is 12,200 feet (3,719 m). The average temperature is 39 degrees Fahrenheit (4°Celsius).

- On average, the world's sea level has risen 4 to 10 inches (10–25 cm) over the last 100 years. Ten thousand years ago, the sea was 330 feet (101 m) lower than it is today. Ten percent of Earth's surface is currently covered in ice. If all the ice at the North and South Pole melted, the world sea level would rise 500 to 600 feet (152–183 m). This increase in water would cover 85 to 90 percent of Earth's surface.

Glossary

coral reefs
Underwater structures made of dead and living coral.

fossil
The remains of an ancient living thing.

lava
Hot material that flows out of a volcano.

monument
A statue or a structure honoring a person or event, or a protected area of land.

orbit
The path an object takes in space around a larger object.

philosopher
A person who thinks about questions or problems facing people.

satellites
Objects that orbit a planet.

submarines
Ships that operate underwater.

turbine
An engine that turns movement into energy.

For More Information

Books

Channing, Margot. *Seas and Oceans*. Mankato, MN: Book House, 2015.

Johnson, Robin. *Oceans Inside Out*. St. Catharine's, Ontario: Crabtree Publishing, 2015.

Wilsdon, Christina. *Ultimate Oceanpedia*. Washington, DC: National Geographic, 2016.

Visit 12StoryLibrary.com

Scan the code or use your school's login at **12StoryLibrary.com** for recent updates about this topic and a full digital version of this book. Enjoy free access to:

- Digital ebook
- Breaking news updates
- Live content feeds
- Videos, interactive maps, and graphics
- Additional web resources

Note to educators: Visit 12StoryLibrary.com/register to sign up for free premium website access. Enjoy live content plus a full digital version of every 12-Story Library book you own for every student at your school.

Index

Alvin, 9, 10, 18–19
animals, 13, 15, 16–17
Atlantis, 9
Atlantis, 22–23

cameras, 9, 11, 16
Cameron, James, 19
Challenger Deep, 5, 6, 11
coral reefs, 15, 19
currents, 14, 25

Deepsea Challenger, 10–11, 19
divers, 6, 10, 12–13, 19, 23, 26
Drebbel, Cornelius, 10
drifters, 14

Exosuit, 13

Gabr, Ahmed, 12
Guam, 7

HMS *Challenger*, 5

mapping, 5, 15
Mariana Trench, 5, 6, 7, 16, 19
Mariana Trench National Monument, 7

National Oceanic and Atmospheric Administration (NOAA), 8, 15
National Wildlife Refuge System, 7

ocean turbines, 24
Okeanos Explorer, 8

Plato, 22

RMS *Titanic*, 10, 18, 19
robots, 9, 12, 26

San Jose, 19
satellites, 14–15
SeaOrbiter, 26–27
sensors, 9, 15
shipwrecks, 18–19, 22
submarines, 5, 9, 10
submersibles, 9, 10, 18–19, 26

Trieste, 5, 11
tsunamis, 20

underwater cities, 22–23
underwater training base, 22

Vikings, 4–5
volcanoes, 20–21

Woods Hole Oceanographic Institute, 9

About the Author
Todd Kortemeier is a writer from Minneapolis, Minnesota. He is a graduate of the University of Minnesota's School of Journalism & Mass Communication. He has authored many books for young people.

READ MORE FROM 12-STORY LIBRARY

Every 12-Story Library book is available in many formats. For more information, visit 12StoryLibrary.com.